MW01226094

PROSPERITY
TEACHERS

Woe to you, teachers of the law and Pharisees, you hypocrites! You clean the outside of the cup and dish, but inside they are full of greed and self-indulgence.

—Jesus

PROSPERITY TEACHERS

The Way of Balaam

They have left the
straight way and wandered
off to follow the way of Balaam son of Beor . . .
—2 Peter 2:15a

Timothy Williams

WINEPRESS WP PUBLISHING

© 2002 by Timothy Williams. All rights reserved

Printed in the United States of America

Published by WinePress Publishing, PO Box 428, Enumclaw, WA 98022.

No part of this publication may be reproduced, stored in a retrieval system, or transmitted in any way by any means—electronic, mechanical, photocopy, recording, or otherwise—without the prior permission of the copyright holder, except as provided by USA copyright law.

Unless otherwise noted, all Scriptures are taken from the Holy Bible, New International Version, © 1973, 1978, 1984 by the International Bible Society. Used by permission of Zondervan Publishing House. The "NIV" and "New International Version" trademarks are registered in the United States Patent and Trademark Office by International Bible Society.

Verses marked NKJV are taken from the New King James Version, © 1979, 1980, 1982 by Thomas Nelson, Inc., Publishers. Used by permission.

ISBN 1-57921-489-4

To the **Point** Series
Ecclesiastes 6:11

Preface

This book is a first in a series of *To The Point* publications, with the purpose of providing teachings that are short, to the point, and require an obedience that comes from faith, (Romans 1:5). This type of obedience, by the power of the Holy Spirit, safeguards all those who love Jesus with an undying love.

The more the words, the less the meaning, and how does that profit anyone? (Ecclesiastes 6:11)

Dedicated to Balaam's donkey which had enough sense to oppose the prophet's madness.

Balaam got up in the morning, saddled his donkey and went with the princes of Moab. But God was very angry when he went, and the angel of the Lord stood in the road to oppose him. Balaam was riding on his donkey, and his two servants were with him. When the donkey saw the angel of the Lord standing in the road with a drawn sword in his hand, she turned off the road into a field. Balaam beat her to get her back on the road. Then the angel of the Lord stood in a narrow path between two vineyards, with walls on both sides. When the donkey saw the angel of the Lord, she pressed close to the wall, crushing Balaam's foot against it. So he beat her again. Then the angel of the Lord moved on ahead and stood in a narrow place where there was no room to turn, either to the right or to the left. When the donkey saw the angel of the Lord, she lay down under Balaam, and he was angry and beat her with his staff. Then the Lord opened the donkey's mouth, and she said to Balaam, "What have I done to make you beat me these three times?" Balaam answered the donkey, "You have made a fool out of me! If I had a sword in my hand, I would kill you right now." The donkey said to Balaam, "Am I not your own donkey, which you have always ridden, to this day? Have I been in the habit of doing this to you?" "No," he said. Then the Lord opened Balaam's eyes, and he saw the angel of the Lord standing in the road with his sword drawn. So he bowed low and fell face-down. The angel of the Lord asked him, "Why have you beaten your donkey these three times? I have come here to oppose you because your path is a reckless one before me. The donkey saw me and turned away from me these three times. If she had not turned away, I would certainly have killed you by now, but I would have spared her." (Numbers 22:21–33)

Contents

The Pharisees, who loved money, heard all this and were sneering at Jesus.

—Matthew 23:25

Cold Times

Because of the increase of wickedness, the love of most will grow cold, but he who stands firm to the end will be saved. (Matthew 24:12–13)

Times are cold, very cold in the Christian church today. Jesus said the love of most would grow cold before His return, and the truth of this surrounds us.[1] One of the greatest signs is the wave of prosperity teachers sweeping the world. Never before in history have there been so many false prophets preaching in the name of Jesus. And, as we shall see, even those who reject these false teachers have more in common with them than first meets the eye.

This short publication is about standing firm against the flood[2] of prosperity teachers who have taken the way of Balaam.

They have left the straight way and wandered off to follow the way of Balaam son of Beor, who loved the wages of wickedness. (2 Peter 2:15)

> **N**ever before in history have there been so many false prophets preaching in the name of Jesus.

The way of Balaam uses God to achieve money, expansion, power and influence. You can read more about Balaam in the book of Numbers or order the free sermon tapes mentioned in the back of the book. These teachers seem to walk very close to the narrow road but "have left the straight way." They can quote Scripture but wander off just enough to make them deadly.

Godliness Is Profitable

Such men believe that "godliness is a means to financial gain." Therefore Paul wrote to Timothy that these men have been "robbed of the truth" and understand "nothing" about Jesus Christ. No matter how much they speak in tongues, or how many books they have sold, or how large their congregations, projects, or how many miracles they perform in Jesus' name, these individuals know zero about the gospel.

> If anyone teaches false doctrines and does not agree to the sound instruction of our Lord Jesus Christ and to godly teaching, he is conceited and understands nothing. He has an unhealthy interest in controversies and quarrels about words that result in envy, strife, malicious talk, evil suspicions and constant friction between men of corrupt mind, who have been robbed of the truth and *who think that godliness is a means to financial gain.* (1 Timothy 6:3–5)

These teachers seem to walk very close to the narrow road but "have left the straight way."

The prosperity teaching states a child of God must learn the laws of prosperity, or "Biblical principals" about success in order to be blessed. In fact, one booklet, entitled "Godliness is Profitable," sums up well the teaching about prosperity.

> "Paul plainly said, 'Godliness is profitable.' If anything is profitable, it pays off. Companies making financial reports to their stockholders list profit and losses. Thank God there is profit from serving God."[3]

What Jesus rebuked, they bless. The way of Balaam encourages people to follow Jesus for the special blessing they will receive. Indeed, they make it so easy to accept Jesus as Savior that all you have to do is say a little prayer.[4] One can only shudder at how many new believers are told that God has something special planned for them in this world. They are never told God's actual plan for them is to make them a slave,[5] and to reduce them to nothing.[6] God's greatest joy was His Son, Jesus, and He wants to make you into that image[7]—holy, clean, poor, weak, dependant, familiar with suffering, and a servant of all. The kind of person the world calls a real loser.[8]

In fact, it is even worse than this. The church seems bent on getting individuals to come to church because they feed their bellies and give them tokens to soothe their flesh. The spirit of Balaam is one of belly belief where people follow God to meet the most basic needs of life, but not really interested in heavenly things for the sake of righteousness. It is an interest in heavenly matters to achieve a selfish goal. When push comes to shove the real reason they go to church is to get something from God, not to place self on the altar of worship. As Philippians 3:19 puts it, *Their destiny is destruction, their god is their stomach, and their glory is in their shame. Their mind is on earthly things.* No wonder so much sexual immorality and decay fills the church today.[9]

> *When push comes to shove the real reason they go to church is to get something from God, not to place self on the altar of worship.*

Again, Jesus rebuked such behavior but the church blesses it in His name. How many come to church only because they receive a little free food, socializing, and entertainment? The church needs to do what Jesus did and tell people the truth of why they really look for Him.

> Jesus answered, "I tell you the truth, you are looking for me, not because you saw miraculous signs but because you ate the loaves and had your fill. (John 6:26)

Woe unto the church that does not rebuke such motives and uses impure methods to increase membership.

The way of Balaam goes beyond money. Individuals are promised health, expanded territory, security, influence, dominion and power. Like such people, Balaam wanted to be a priest of God but didn't want to give up his selfishness to be holy.

One of the key verses quoted by every person embracing the spirit of Balaam is 3 John 2.

> Beloved, I pray that you may prosper in all things and be in health, just as your soul prospers. (3 John 2 NKJV)

To "prosper" is twisted to mean worldly advancement. To be in good health is interpreted to mean that sickness and poverty are signs of weak faith and sin. Prosperity teachers cannot fathom how the gospel could win converts any other way. They have forgotten that God's ways are not our ways and it should not surprise them that God's idea of prosperity totally differs from man's. For example, if God does heal or work a miracle it is so that we might die more to self. Look at Paul, a man stoned to death, raised from the dead so that he might go to the next town to suffer and die for Jesus.

They have forgotten that God's ways are not our ways and it should not surprise them that God's idea of prosperity totally differs from man's.

> Then some Jews came from Antioch and Iconium and won the crowd over. They stoned Paul and dragged him outside the city, thinking he was dead. But after the disciples had gathered around him, he got up and went back into the city. The next day he and Barnabas left for Derbe. (Acts 14:19–20)

The Prosperity of Jesus

There is only one kind of blessed prosperity. For a correct understanding of this passage—and all passages—we must return to the offensive message of the cross.[10] Only then will a man see that what John meant by "prosper" is that we advance in the will of God, leading a crucified life and dying to self by suffering in our body to be done with sin.[11] It might include becoming sick and poor so that the gospel can advance. In fact, Paul writes in Galatians 4:13, "As you know, it was because of an illness that I first preached the gospel to you." We must understand that God's idea of prosper is different than the world's. Let us read Isaiah 53:10 and see how God views prosperity.

> Yet it was the Lord's will to crush him and cause him to suffer, and though the Lord makes his life a guilt offering, he will see his offspring and prolong his days, and the will of the Lord will prosper in his hand. (Isaiah 53:10)

Do you see that God's idea of "prosper" is to "cause him to suffer," to "crush him?" If this is God's idea of prosperity for His beloved Son, then when He prospers us with holiness and obedience, it will look the same. After all, Jesus didn't die on the cross so we could prosper in the world according to the world's standards. Otherwise the example Jesus set would have been one of a land baron giving away millions of dollars to others.

The bottom line is that the Bible is not talking at all about worldly prosperity. Indeed, as we shall see, God declares the opposite. Let us all pray to be rescued from such wicked men whose prosperity or reward is "in this life."

O Lord, by your hand save me from such men, from men of this

> After all, Jesus didn't die on the cross so we could prosper in the world according to the world's standards. Otherwise the example Jesus set would have been one of a land baron giving away millions of dollars to others.

world whose *reward is in this life.* You still the hunger of those you cherish; their sons have plenty, and they store up wealth for their children. (Psalms 17:14)

> **P**aul definitely knew hunger, sickness, and poverty. Shall we slander him by saying this happened because of his lack of faith?

True enough, someday the wealth of the wicked will be given to the righteous—but not until Jesus returns.[12] The "hunger" and "wealth" David sung of and Jesus taught does not concern physical food and wealth in this life.[13] Truly God will end all hunger,[14] and wealth is stored up in heaven for children if their parents have lived a righteous life. No greater inheritance can a parent leave than true righteousness, that is true riches.[15] If the bread for the flesh is absent, God will give the bread of life to sustain us through the suffering. Thus, while God does not always give relief the way we want, we will never really hunger if we lay down our lives for Him.

> **I**n this world, the Bible declares, we will not prosper. Only in heaven will we rest assured that we will not hunger or hurt.

God calls all disciples to become servants and the possibility that He (not the devil) works the sufferings of Jesus in our lives is a firm reality.[16] Paul definitely knew hunger, sickness, and poverty. Shall we slander him by saying this happened because of his lack of faith? In addition, let us not forget that we are "considered as sheep to be slaughtered" for the sake of the gospel.[17] If these things were true for Paul, a great saint of God, how can we be exempt from them?[18]

Rather, as servants of God we commend ourselves in every way: in great endurance; in troubles, hardships and distresses; in beatings, imprisonments and riots; in hard work, sleepless nights and hunger; . . . (2 Corinthians 6:4–5)

I have labored and toiled and have often gone without sleep; I have known hunger and thirst and have often gone without food; I have been cold and naked. (2 Corinthians 11:27)

In this world, the Bible declares, we will not prosper. Only in heaven will we rest assured that we will not hunger or hurt.[19] To put another nail in the coffin of the prosperity doctrine let us read from the book of Hebrews and see what kind of faith God commends.[20]

> Instead of fine suits, they wore sheepskins. Instead of fancy dresses, they wore goatskins. Instead of taking the city for Jesus, they were sawed in two.

They were stoned; they were sawed in two; they were put to death by the sword. They went about in sheepskins and goatskins, destitute, persecuted and mistreated—the world was not worthy of them. They wandered in deserts and mountains, and in caves and holes in the ground. (Hebrews 11:37–38)

"The world was not worthy of them," and it showed by how they did not prosper in this world. Instead of fine suits, they wore sheepskins. Instead of fancy dresses, they wore goatskins. Instead of taking the city for Jesus, they were sawed in two. Instead of increasing in wealth, they wandered in deserts and mountains. Instead of a new church building, they lived in caves and holes in the ground. The man or church that prospers in this world will not be found worthy of the world to come. For those who pros-

> For those who prosper in this world have embraced it and are loved by this world. By this one fact, they have proven themselves enemies of God.

per in this world have embraced it and are loved by this world.[21] By this one fact, they have proven themselves enemies of God.[22] After all Satan only rewards his own while forcing the children of God to make bricks without straw.[23]

Blackest Darkness

So vile is the way of Balaam that God will place such individuals in the blackest, darkest part of hell. God reserves a special spot in hell for those who use the way of Balaam to grow a church or ministry. That spot is dark, very dark. It contains a blackness they will feel and not be able to see the tormenting flames.[24] There, prosperity teachers will grope in utter darkness while the putrid smell of sulfur fills their nostrils.

> *So vile is the way of Balaam that God will place such individuals in the blackest, darkest part of hell.*

Blackest darkness is reserved for them. (2 Peter 2:17)

> *Like Judas, prosperity teachers want silver coins, influence, or power out of their association with Jesus.*

God will do this because they deserve it—they preached darkness as if it were light.[25] These teachers took His name and used it to promise others worldly blessings. They broke the command not to misuse the name of the Lord.[26] Like Balaam and Judas these teachers thought they could get something out of the deal for themselves as they followed God. They both hung around God, hoping to get something, but their true motives became evident. Like Judas, prosperity teachers want silver coins, influence, or power out of their association with Jesus. They talk of helping the poor, but it is only themselves they are concerned with. In short, they use the poor to further their ministry and lusts.

What Satan has done is lift these ministries up in numbers, pride and works and then whispered in their ears that they are children of the King.

> But one of his disciples, Judas Iscariot, who was later to betray him, objected, "Why wasn't this perfume sold and the money given to the poor? It was worth a year's wages." He did not say this because he cared about the poor but because he was a thief; as keeper of the money bag, he used to help himself to what was put into it. (John 12:4–6)

They talk of being blessed that they might be a blessing, but such double talk is a lie. They only want to be blessed and are willing to use the needs of the poor to get what they want. It is some of the most unloving double-talk a man can speak. How utterly wicked of a man to use selflessness to gain for himself. It is the very heart of Judas speaking through a prosperity teacher and believer.

Like Satan did to Jesus, he bids them to jump into the promises of God. The difference is the prosperity person jumps and Jesus rebukes.

They even boast of speaking the Word of God but do not realize it is the spirit of Satan quoting the Bible. What Satan has done is lift these ministries up in numbers, pride and works and then whispered in their ears that they are children of the King. It is the same temptation Satan used on Jesus, the only difference is they embrace the temptation as a being from God. Notice on the next page that Satan puts Jesus on the "highest point of the temple" and then

> They will tell you that David and Solomon had riches—but they will not tell you that David did not enjoy these riches and Solomon found them meaningless.

quotes Scripture. Satan quoted, in context, a portion of Psalm 91. Satan speaks of God's love, concern and care for Jesus just as he does through the prosperity teacher to the congregation. But it is all a trick. Satan tells the prosperity person they are children of the King, the world is theirs and all they need do is claim it. Like Satan did to Jesus, he bids them to jump into the promises of God. The difference is the prosperity person jumps and Jesus rebukes.

> Then the devil took him to the holy city and had him stand on the highest point of the temple. "If you are the Son of God," he said, "throw yourself down. For it is written: "'He will command his angels concerning you, and they will lift you up in their hands, so that you will not strike your foot against a stone.'" (Matthew 4:5–6)

Such men are "experts in greed." They know how to sling sermons in such a way that greed in the name of the Lord seems noble. They will tell you that David and Solomon had riches—but they will not tell you that David did not enjoy these riches and Solomon found them meaningless.[27] They will not tell you that kings, whether a king of the Old Testament or children of the King today, were commanded not to collect wealth.[28] That pastors, as Levites, are not to own land or be known for the homes and things they own. They are to invoke blessings upon other people but they are not to accumulate those blessings for themselves.

> At that time the Lord set apart the tribe of Levi to carry the ark of the covenant of the Lord, to stand before the Lord to minister and to pronounce blessings in his name, as they still do today. That is why the Levites have no share or inheritance among their brothers; the

> God's method is never to bless us that we might bless others.

Lord is their inheritance, as the Lord your God told them. (Deuteronomy 10:8–9)

The Levites received no share of the land but only towns to live in, with pasturelands for their flocks and herds. (Joshua 14:4)

God's method is never to bless us that we might bless others. God's method is to crucify us and through our poverty and weakness we might bless others. Below are listed just a few examples.

> How many try to hold God hostage with His Word, thinking if they know the Word, have faith and step out in those things that God must answer.

Sorrowful, yet always rejoicing; poor, yet making many rich; having nothing, and yet possessing everything. (2 Corinthians 6:10)

Out of the most severe trial, their overflowing joy and their extreme poverty welled up in rich generosity. (2 Corinthians 8:2)

The prosperity church, even with all of its talk about miracles, cannot say with Peter, "Silver or gold I do not have . . ."

Peter looked straight at him, as did John. Then Peter said, "Look at us!" So the man gave them his attention, expecting to get something from them. Then Peter said, "Silver or gold I do not have, but what I have I give you. In the name of Jesus Christ of Nazareth, walk." (Acts 3:4–6)

They do not understand that wanting anything more than daily food and clothing denotes greed in God's sight.[29] "With eyes full of adultery" they always look for some new way to commit adultery against the Lord by embracing the world.

With eyes full of adultery, they never stop sinning; they seduce the unstable; they are experts in greed—an accursed brood! They have left the straight way and wandered off to follow the way of

> Balaam son of Beor, who loved the wages of wickedness. But he
> was rebuked for his wrongdoing by a donkey—a beast without
> speech—who spoke with a man's voice and restrained the
> prophet's madness. (2 Peter 2:14–16)

Think about it. A donkey had more insight and obedience than
Balaam. To press for obedience among those filled with the spirit
of Balaam is to suffer their wrath. Just as Balaam beat his donkey
because he could not get what he wanted, so too these individuals
beat against the Word of God. It is madness without a shred of
reason. They have forgotten that when they invoke the blessings
or the promises of the Bible, but refuse to die to self, every curse
falls upon them. Indeed, God will "blot out" their name from the
book of life.

When we claim promises without true death to self we put God to
the test. We seek to box Him in so that He must deliver the promise. So many try to hold God hostage with His Word, thinking if
they know the Word, have faith and step out in those things that
God will answer. They invoke the blessings of God's Word but live
for themselves and thus will reap, not prosperity, but, all the curses
that are in the Bible.

> When such a person hears the words of this oath, he invokes a
> blessing on himself and therefore thinks, "I will be safe, even
> though I persist in *going my own way.*" This will bring disaster
> on the watered land as well as the dry. The Lord will never be
> willing to forgive him; his wrath and zeal will burn against
> that man. All the curses written in this book will fall upon
> him, and the Lord will blot out his name from under heaven.
> (Deuteronomy 29:19–20, emphasis added)

Indeed, God declares that He will search out the prosperity indi-
vidual and insure their judgment. Not only will God "never be
willing to forgive him" but God will "single him out" to curse the
prosperity teacher. As we have seen, God will single out such men
and place them in the darkest blackest part of hell to be tortured.

The Lord will single him out from all the tribes of Israel for disaster, according to all the curses of the covenant written in this Book of the Law. (Deuteronomy 29:21)

Simply put, you cannot, as the prosperity people do, go your own way with self alive and expect not to be judged. Woe unto those who quote Scripture, applying those Scriptures to themselves without a suffering, offensive cross having first put them to death!

> *Prosperity teachers obtain their power and influence because the church has become increasingly selfish in the name of Jesus. They, along with most churches today, use the lust of the flesh to gain members.*

It is not just prosperity teachers who enjoy the lie. Many a Bible college, ministry and author dabble with Balaam's madness.[30] The current twisted use of the prayer of Jabez provides abundant proof.[31]

The prosperity teacher is like a mirror reflecting the face of the gazer. Such teachers mirror back what hides in people's hearts.[32] Therefore Scripture declares that in these days, the last days, men will "not put up with sound doctrine. Instead, to suit their own desires, they will gather around them a *great number* of teachers to say what their itching ears want to hear" (2 Timothy 4:3, emphasis added). All because men love themselves instead of God. Now loving self is justified if we can say with our lips that the goal is to help others. The art of being self-centered is now painted with colorful strokes of the brush.

> *They appeal to the "lustful desires of sinful human nature" to entice people to come to church. After all, who doesn't want to have an abundance and take authority over the world?*

But mark this: There will be terrible times in the last days. People will be lovers of themselves . . . (2 Timothy 3:1–2)

Chapter 3

Appealing to the Flesh

Prosperity teachers obtain their power and influence because the church has become increasingly selfish in the name of Jesus. They, along with most churches today, use the lust of the flesh to gain members. From Cappuccino machines to unholy music, millions are drawn to churches by blatant appeals to the flesh. Churches promise "freedom" as they boast they are children of the King.

> *The way of Balaam wins influence by giving individuals what their flesh desires,*

Everything is joyful, happy and worth celebrating. It is golden calf worship done in the name of the Lord, (see Exodus 32). The offense, judgment and death to self is not preached, understood and accepted. Because of this they forfeit the true resurrected life. They appeal to the "lustful desires of sinful human nature" to entice people to come to church. After all, who doesn't want to have an abundance and take authority over the world? So in order to gain a following, they "mouth empty, boastful words" of how they have the truth and the power. In reality, they are "slaves of depravity." They just know how to make depravity look godly.

Until a man picks up the true cross of Christ, he will never fully see through such perversion. He might point the finger at their excesses and foolishness, but he will have no real insight into the core of the sin. Most "discernment ministries" fall into this category.

As you listen to the prosperity teacher preach it is easy to pick up on their emptiness and boasting. They continually claim and promise things and poke fun at the Devil.

> For they mouth empty, boastful words and, by appealing to the lustful desires of sinful human nature, they entice people who are just escaping from those who live in error. They promise them freedom, while they themselves are slaves of depravity—for a man is a slave to whatever has mastered him. (2 Peter 2:18–19)

The way of Balaam wins influence by giving individuals what their flesh desires, "by appealing to the lustful desires of sinful human nature." This is the test for all churches, ministries, books, seminars, camps, events, musicians, and worship teams. If they appeal to the flesh and do not preach an offensive message of the cross, it is the spirit of Balaam at work. They promise fun, food, wisdom, and a whitewash for sin in their lives. This occurs not only in their lives, but also in the sermons and even the music they find acceptable.[33] They win over those who are "just escaping" by telling them what their flesh wants to hear.[34] Like Balaam, they know what will work to cut off those lagging behind in obeying God.[35]

When one listens to the TV shows, the radio programs and pulpits today what you hear is a flattery feast. Each person tells the other person how godly and great they will become as God uses them.

Who doesn't want to be out of debt? Who wouldn't want to be well all the time or have things go smoothly in this world? Who doesn't want a mes-

Jesus did not promise us fun or an easy road in this world—quite the opposite.

sage that promises the curse is lifted and all kinds of good things will come their way? Who wouldn't want to have a lot of fun and still go to heaven? Who doesn't want to be told they are great and will become even greater? It is the same appeal to pride that the Serpent used with Eve, and God's perfection and righteousness is perverted to mean we become righteous. It is a use of flattery that

> Without this suffering, no one can go to heaven and no one can be saved.

deceives many. When one listens to the TV shows, the radio programs and pulpits today what you hear is a flattery feast. Each person tells the other person how godly and great they will become as God uses them. How easily they deceive those "naive" about the true gospel of the cross.

> For such people are not serving our Lord Christ, but their own appetites. By smooth talk and flattery they deceive the minds of naive people. (Romans 16:18)

> The Bible gives no 1-2-3, quick-and-easy, ask-Jesus-in-your-heart-and-go-to-heaven gospel.

This is the same message the snake offered Eve in the Garden of Eden—the pleasing of her flesh along with being like God. The prosperity teachers also promise god-likeness while feeding the flesh of their audience.

But at least the snake didn't do it in the name of God. Therefore God reserves the blackest part of hell for such individuals and ministries. Better that they were honest and offered to feed the sin of others with clarity than to use the name of Jesus to lure people to church. Better that they came in the name of Satan than to come in the name of Jesus.

Co-heirs with Christ

Jesus did not promise us fun or an easy road in this world—quite the opposite. Jesus told us we must walk like He did, carrying a cross, hating our lives, and denying self. Sure, this sounds hard, for it is a "hard teaching."[36] On the other hand, there is nothing hard about the prosperity teaching.

Indeed, the Bible teaches that if we want to reign with Jesus we must first suffer. Without this suffering, no one can go to heaven and no one can be saved. We cannot be "co-heirs with Christ" unless we "indeed share in his sufferings in order that we may also share in his glory." The Bible gives no 1-2-3, quick-and-easy, ask-Jesus-in-your-heart-and-go-to-heaven gospel.[37]

Only those who can see past the glitter of gold, the lure of money, power, and influence have a saving faith in Jesus. For they have not been polluted by the ways of the world.

> Now if we are children, then we are heirs—heirs of God and co-heirs with Christ, if indeed we share in his sufferings in order that we may also share in his glory. (Romans 8:17)

Many ask, "How then can we get people to come to church if we preach such a 'negative' gospel?" The answer is as old as the gospel itself. It is by faith and seeing beyond the world. Just as Jesus showed us that the life of faith is doing God's will for the "joy set before Him," we too must endure the sufferings of the cross that we might share in the joys of heaven for all eternity. This is why God tells us to "fix our eyes on Jesus." Only those who can see past the glitter of gold, the lure of money, power, and influence have a saving faith in Jesus. For they have not been polluted by the ways of the world.[38]

We are never to get people saved, but are only to allow the Holy Spirit to move upon their hearts.[39] People must get saved in spite of the sufferings of the cross—not because we lure them into church by giving them fun things to do or believe. It is not our job to draw people to church, that is the work of the Holy Spirit. We are only to lift up a crucified Jesus, with all that means, and allow the Holy Spirit to draw who it can.[40] We are to plant and water, but we cannot make things grow.[41]

"Now is the time for judgment on this world; now the prince of this world will be driven out. But I, when I am lifted up from the earth, will draw all men to myself." (John 12:31–32)

> *You have to give them credit, they are good at making greed seem godly.*

The world should see a joy in being crucified to self. After all, the good news is that you can be dead to who you are. Just as Jesus lived,[42] we must preach and teach other disciples what to do; to become losers in this world[43] and hate our own lives for the "joy set before" us. Now is our time of testing, a time to endure the cross.[44] And only after we have passed the test will we sit down with Jesus.[45]

Let us fix our eyes on Jesus, the author and perfecter of our faith, who for the joy set before him endured the cross, scorning its shame, and sat down at the right hand of the throne of God. (Hebrews 12:2)

When a prosperity teacher or any church gains members by feeding the flesh, they give these followers a faith based on man and Satan, not upon God. They may claim their faith is in God, but its power comes from a man who simply persuaded someone to come to church.[46] This is something wicked in the sight of God and no different than any other club, political party, or sporting event.

Chapter 4

Despising Dung

Would you give your child a bowl of dung for breakfast? Of course not. So why would you expect God to bless you financially? Money is a "detestable" thing to God. We should not then expect God to bless us with something He finds detestable. Money is "highly valued among men," but to quote it once again, it "is detestable in God's sight."

> The Pharisees, who loved money, heard all this and were sneering at Jesus. He said to them, "You are the ones who justify yourselves in the eyes of men, but God knows your hearts. What is highly valued among men is detestable in God's sight. (Luke 16:14–15)

Those following the way of Balaam "sneer" at the attitude of simple obedience to Jesus' call for us to "hate" and "despise" money. Such prosperity teachers know how to "justify themselves in the eyes of men." They can sling the logic, say the prayers,

> *There is only one proper perspective on money and one test that determines if a man loves money or not. The point Jesus made was simple. Those who do not hate money, love it.*

> True Christians simply share everything they have out of love. A people touched by the Holy Spirit and the cross do not prosper in a worldly way, they share everything they have until they become poor.

and show the material goods to prove their points. You have to give them credit, they are good at making greed seem godly. But every church committee and ministry that does not hate and despise money bows down to worship it—there is no middle ground.

"No one can serve two masters. Either he will hate the one and love the other, or he will be devoted to the one and despise the other. You cannot serve both God and Money." (Matthew 6:24)

> It is utter folly to believe that God grants the desires of our heart without our having first been crucified to that desire.

The problem with judging a prosperity ministry is that even those who reject such teachings need to judge themselves first—for they also do not know how to hate and despise money. We must come to realize by the light of the Holy Spirit that those who do not hate money love it.

• Until we come to understand that a good steward of money gives away all, we are in danger of the prosperity teaching.[47]

• Until we realize that a good budget will never work in Jesus, we remain unprepared for the bread of life.[48]

• Until we are dead to the joy of getting the best price for something, we cannot say we are filled with the Holy Spirit.[49]

• Until we surrender our little nest egg to a cross that takes all, we are not fit for working in the cause of Christ.[50]

- Until we are ready to throw away the financial planning books, we are not ready to pick up the Bible or our cross.[51]

- Until we can say, "I hate money." We are not worthy to speak against the prosperity teachers.[52]

- Until we stop claiming things in Jesus and start praying according to God's will, we are unworthy to utter one single word in prayer.[53]

- Until we stop "sneering" at God about the need to both hate and despise money, we will not really see through the prosperity teacher.[54]

How wicked Christians have become. The world is more wise in its use of money than the church.[55] Those that should be the most giving, are more stingy than the world. The Christian church should be showing the world how to hate and despise worldly goods and money, but by being tight fisted and claiming the world as it's own, the church shows the world how to be greedy.

Usually, to justify our greed, we quote 1 Timothy 6:10 and say something like, "But the Bible says it is the *love* of money that is a sin, not money itself." Our spin, twist, and justification that "we don't love money but have it in a proper perspective" is a sham. There is only one proper perspective on money and one test that determines if a man loves money or not. The point Jesus made was simple. Those who do not hate money, love it. Those who do not despise wealth, love it. According to God, if you do not both hate and despise money then 1 Timothy 6:10 applies to you—you are a lover of money.

The test for 1 Timothy is Matthew 6:24. The tougher Scripture always gives the understanding for the "easier" verse because both the gate and the road are narrow. Most people, in their sinful folly, apply Scripture backwards. They see the demands of the tough

Scripture and search through the Bible to undo the pressure. They commit the void factor. They use God against Himself voiding out what one Scripture states in order to widen the narrow road. One can only shudder at how angry God will be at a people who twist His words back at Him. No doubt He will be full of rage.

> A true Christian spends his last coin, by the strength of his last breath, to meet the needs of Jesus.

Money is a detestable thing, the very opposite of love. God did not invent money, nor would godly people value money. They would, like the first church, claim nothing as their own.[56] True Christians simply share everything they have out of love.[57] A people touched by the Holy Spirit and the cross do not prosper in a worldly way, they share everything they have until they become poor.[58] How quickly we have forgotten Lot's wife[59] and fail to use "worldly wealth" to "gain friends" rather than to fill our personal pockets. How many are like Judas who "helped himself to what was put into the money bag." (John 12:6)

Desires of the Heart

> Delight yourself in the Lord and he will give you the desires of your heart. (Psalm 37:4)

> You want to be rich in God? Then deny self and give away all you can, making yourself poor like Jesus.

Today the preaching about money uses the old saying the "ends justify the means." In other words, if you ask for wealth because you want to help others, then your prayers magically become acceptable. Such noble sounding words set up a smoke screen for a greedy heart that may deceive ourselves and others, but not God.[60] As the people reacted in Jeremiah's day to God's truth,[61] so prosperity teachers today live a lie. It is utter folly to believe that God grants the desires of our heart without our having first been crucified to that desire. Unless your heart has been dealt a death blow by God, He will not grant you a thing except judgment and wrath. Such was the situation when God gave the Israelites meat. The Bible declares that God's anger broke out against them while the meat remained in their mouths.[62] So it is true that individuals have proof of many answered prayers, but it is God's judgment being worked out. God is very shrewd toward the crooked. He knows how to answer their prayers and, depending on their heart's response, it either works God's wrath or a humility in them that admits its folly in asking.

> . . . to the pure you show yourself pure, but to the crooked you show yourself shrewd. (Psalms 18:26)

Our hearts are "deceitful above all things." Indeed, it cannot be cured, it can only be killed.[63] And until death to self has been experienced in a painful practical way, God will not, cannot, give us the desires of our hearts. For to do so would be to bless wickedness. The prosperity person should never utter a prayer until the cross has first crucified their flesh.[64] And it is a daily cross we are called to carry that must crucify our wicked hearts every hour of every day. Unless this is happening we are not able to hear the voice of the Holy Spirit.

In fact, if I gave you a bag of dung—something detestable—you would want to get rid of it as quickly as possible. And that was exactly Jesus' point. The goal of every true disciple is to die broke, having given away all, and to enter heaven saying of worldly wealth, "It is gone."

> I tell you, use worldly wealth to gain friends for yourselves, so that *when it is gone,* you will be welcomed into eternal dwellings. (Luke 16:9, emphasis added)

Let all true saints pray the humble prayer of Proverbs instead of embracing the prosperity madness of Balaam.

A true Christian spends his last coin, by the strength of his las breath, to meet the needs of Jesus.[65] Is your idea of prosperity to advance in the likeness of Jesus, to increase in proverty, to make yourself poor as Jesus did? Remembering that we are to walk a Jesus walked.[66]

> For you know the grace of our Lord Jesus Christ, that though he was rich, yet for your sakes he became poor, so that you through his poverty might become rich. (2 Corinthians 8:9)

As the verse above shows us, this is the "grace of our Lord." A grace that out of love, for the sake of others, makes itself "poor." This i why James builds on this point by telling us that the poor should boast that they remain "high" on God's list of favorite people. While the rich man who prospers should go around boasting of his "low position on God's list. The rich are never to be the first chosen for leadership in the church. They have a low position in Christ.

> The brother in humble circumstances ought to take pride in his high position. But the one who is rich should take pride in his low position, because he will pass away like a wild flower. (James 1:9–10)

True prosperity is found in being unconcerned about the things of this world and quietly trusting God to work His will in a person's life.

There remains no proper balance toward worldly prosperity, but only the cross that works a hatred and despising of it. There is only God and the Cross.[67] A God who bids u to hate our own lives, despise th dollar, give up all, deny ourselves suffer for His sake, and become poor by following Jesus. After all we know it is more blessed to give than to receive.[68] You want to be rich in God? Then deny self and give away all you can,[69] mak ing yourself poor like Jesus.[70]

Every Scripture about money or wealth must be understood from the cross of Christ. The Holy Spirit must make the issue of despis ing the dollar alive in us by way of a crucified life. Otherwise we will misinterpret every Scripture and fall prey to false teachers—be that the most conservative Baptist preacher that feeds the flesh to draw a crowd, or the woman selling prosperity doctrine on the television.

Finally, let us conclude this section by hearing Jesus tell us that worldly wealth is not true riches. In one bold statement Jesus tells us two powerful things. First, if we do not hate and despise money, God cannot truly bless us. And secondly, worldly wealth is not the "true riches" that God blesses us with. Indeed, it is the worldly wealth Jesus tells us by contrast that is of no value at all.

> So if you have not been trustworthy in handling worldly wealth, who will trust you with true riches? (Luke 16:11)

Let all true saints pray the humble prayer of Proverbs instead of embracing the prosperity madness of Balaam. Let every prosperity believer claim this promise and pray this prayer every day if they want to be blessed as God blesses. This will "keep falsehood and lies" far from them. The man who prays for more than daily food is wide open for falsehood and lies. He will be taken in every time by false teachers and schemers.

> Keep falsehood and lies far from me; give me neither poverty nor riches, but give me only my daily bread. (Proverbs 30:8)

What are riches according to Proverbs? Having more than your daily bread. What is poverty? Having no bread at all for the day. Most of us want far more than this and pray way beyond what is allowed by God.

True Prosperity

True prosperity is found in being unconcerned about the things of this world and quietly trusting God to work His will in a person's life. It is a "secret" few ever really discover. Most are unwilling to be taught that they might learn the secret of contentment.

> I know what it is to be in need, and I know what it is to have plenty. I have learned the secret of being content in any and every situation, whether well fed or hungry, whether living in plenty or in want. I can do everything through him who gives me strength. (Philippians 4:12–13)

> *As a preacher, I cannot promise you that you will be lifted out of your poverty in this world. What I can promise is if you seek God with a loving heart He will never leave or forsake you.*

When Paul speaks of God's power he means the power to be content- that is true prosperity in this world. If someone is poor, they have the power to trust God for daily needs. And if someone has plenty, to be dead to that and giving abundantly on all occasions.[71] When we pray we are not to pray about more land, cars, homes, and success in this world. In fact, Jesus tells us to remember Lot's wife who turned back to look at the world because there was something she did not want to leave behind. The lesson of Lot's wife is that we must be a people totally unconcerned with the things and ways of this world.[72] Not only are we not to worry about such things, but we should simply pray about daily bread and leave the rest to God's will and direction.

> So do not worry, saying, 'What shall we eat?' or 'What shall we drink?' or 'What shall we wear?' For the pagans run after all these things, and your heavenly Father knows that you need them. But seek first his kingdom and his righteousness, and all these things will be given to you as well. (Matthew 6:31–33)

That daily bread might include physical bread to eat or the bread of life that will sustain us when we are hungry. Again, when Jesus taught us to pray He taught us only to ask for our "daily bread" and not worry about the rest.

Give us each day our daily bread. (Luke 11:3)

The man who is able to trust God, content to let the world and its things go by, is very rich indeed. Such a man will prosper with the Lord and in the end receive comfort that was denied him by the selfishness of the prosperity preacher. All who claim to be disciples of Jesus would do well to read this passage slowly and carefully until the Holy Spirit drives us to tears.

> "There was a rich man who was dressed in purple and fine linen and lived in luxury every day. At his gate was laid a beggar named Lazarus, covered with sores and longing to eat what fell from the rich man's table. Even the dogs came and licked his sores. The time came when the beggar died and the angels carried him to Abraham's side. The rich man also died and was buried. In hell, where he was in torment, he looked up and saw Abraham far away, with Lazarus by his side. So he called to him, 'Father Abraham, have pity on me and send Lazarus to dip the tip of his finger in water and cool my tongue, because I am in agony in this fire.' But Abraham replied, 'Son, remember that in your lifetime you received your good things, while Lazarus received bad things, but now he is comforted here and you are in agony.'" (Luke 16:19–25)

Woe unto the prosperity preachers, teachers, followers, and all who do not hate and despise money. Woe unto them because they grind the faces of the poor in the dust by their wicked doctrines. They give them

Anyone who claims to be a Christian but remains greedy and unrepentant must be judged and rejected.

doctrines and promises that will end in delusion and even greater poverty. They prey upon their poverty to gain a following and use the poor for their own selfish gain. All true disciples must denounce and disfellowship themselves from these elders, leaders, and false prophets who are ruining God's vineyard.

The Lord enters into judgment against the elders and leaders of his people: "It is you who have ruined my vineyard; the plunder from the poor is in your houses. What do you mean by crushing my people and grinding the faces of the poor?" declares the Lord, the Lord Almighty. The Lord says, "The women of Zion are haughty, walking along with outstretched necks, flirting with their eyes, tripping along with mincing steps, with ornaments jingling on their ankles." (Isaiah 3:14–16)

Did you notice the last part of that passage and how haughty the women are? You will notice the same among women prosperity preachers. Everything about their actions, dress, and manners speak of haughtiness and mincing steps. Indeed, they even rebel against God's clear command not to teach men.[73]

From the twisted use of the prayer of Jabez, to ministries that pride themselves on pointing out such falsehoods, the love of self sends forth its stench.

As a preacher, I cannot promise you that you will be lifted out of your poverty in this world. What I can promise is if you seek God with a loving heart He will never leave or forsake you.[74] His love will always abound in your heart even if it does not go well with your life. Seek first His kingdom and God will supply all that you need for He is a loving God.

> So do not worry, saying, 'What shall we eat?' or 'What shall we drink?' or 'What shall we wear?' For the pagans run after all these things, and your heavenly Father knows that you need them. But seek first his kingdom and his righteousness, and all these things will be given to you as well. Therefore do not worry about tomorrow, for tomorrow will worry about itself. Each day has enough trouble of its own. (Matthew 6:31–34)

You cannot eat at the table of demons and the table of the Lord at the same time.

Nor can I promise the rich that they will remain rich. Indeed, if you are rich I command you to be generous and stop thinking you are right with God because you are rich.[75]

What to Do

Anyone who claims to be a Christian but remains greedy and un-repentant must be judged and rejected. Indeed, Jesus said we must give up "everything" before we can even say we belong to Him.[76] Do you know someone that claims to be a believer but does not hate and despise money? Then you must warn them. And, if they will not re-pent, you should not even eat lunch with them. You cannot "associate" with them at church or in public. They must be denounced, shamed, and fully rejected or you shall share in their most awful of judgments.

> If we are open to the leading of the Holy Spirit, we will hear that voice telling us to call such people to repentance—immediate repentance.

But now I am writing you that you must not associate with any-one who calls himself a brother but is sexually immoral or greedy, an idolater or a slanderer, a drunkard or a swindler. With such a man do not even eat. (1 Corinthians 5:11)

Unless a church knows how to preach and live a message where individuals hate[77] their own lives and despise money, they stand in league with the prosperity teachers. Let it be fully understood that the way of Balaam even sweeps in among churches that oppose the prosperity teaching. What has replaced selfless love for Jesus is, in reality, a love for self in the name of Jesus. These are the "terrible times" God warned us would come to the church. Such is the current state of the church, where we find a "form of godliness" but people's lives and deceptive love of self causes them to deny the power of God.[78] They deny His power by their actions of not honestly carrying a cross. As Titus 1:16 tells us, "They claim to know God, but by their actions they deny him. They are detestable, disobedient and unfit for doing anything good." Few know the power of a cross that causes one to suffer in their body to overcome sin.[79]

> But mark this: There will be terrible times in the last days. People will be lovers of themselves, lovers of money, boastful, proud, abusive, disobedient to their parents, ungrateful, unholy, without love, unforgiving, slanderous, without self-control, brutal, not lovers of the good, treacherous, rash, conceited, lovers of pleasure rather than lovers of God—having a form of godliness but denying its power . . . (2 Timothy 3:1–5)

From the twisted use of the prayer of Jabez, to ministries that pride themselves on pointing out such falsehoods, the love of self sends forth its stench. From churches that provide fun and entertaining sermons[80] to those who rebuke such shallowness, the love of self reigns supreme. Indeed, the spiritual insanity that sweeps the church is proof enough that most are in love with themselves.[81]

Jesus said that if we obey His teaching, we will remain in His love. If we want to remain in that love we must obey and withdraw all fellowship from those who embrace any form, whether by life or doctrine, of the prosperity teaching.

If you obey my commands, you will remain in my love, just as I have obeyed my Father's commands and remain in his love. (John 15:10)

If we fail to obey God in this matter because we seek to "love" or show favoritism to someone we care about, we endanger the love of God in our own lives. You cannot eat at the table of demons and the table of the Lord at the same time.

We have seen that the way God would have us deal with a prosperity teacher or follower is through disfellowship. If we are open to the leading of the Holy Spirit, we will hear that voice telling us to call such people to repentance—immediate repentance. If someone you know follows a prosperity teacher, you must gently warn him of his error and if they will not repent that day, have nothing further to do with them. If you find yourself in the company of a prosperity teacher or prophet, renounce them publicly as Jesus did the Pharisees.

Let us pause for just a moment and examine a couple of last points about these individuals.

These men are springs without water and mists driven by a storm. Blackest darkness is reserved for them. (2 Peter 2:17)

2 Peter 2:17 warns us, they are "springs without water and mists driven by a storm." Displaying all the energy, lightening, noise, and wind of a thunderstorm their events, promises, preaching, miracles, and false doctrines blow into churches. They demonstrate a whirlwind of shouting, dancing, clapping, laughter, miracles, entertainment, and self exaltation. Their ads and announcements promise blessings, life, happiness, and excitement. At first they appear to have some life, for they are a "mist" of water vapor that promises an eternal spring, but like a fog it hides the path of life. In fact, the prosperity doctrine will put someone, as repeated earlier, in the "blackest darkness" part of hell.

God is very clear. There is only one way every true Christian and church should respond to those following the way of Balaam, whether it be Mom, Dad, friend, or favorite preacher, they must have nothing to do with them. Nothing!

. . . Have nothing to do with them. (2 Timothy 3:5)

. . . Therefore do not be partners with them. (Ephesians 5:7)

. . . With such a man do not even eat. (1 Corinthians 5:11)

. . . Leave them; they are blind guides. (Matthew 15:14)

———————————— ✽ ————————————

Blessed is the man
who does not walk in the counsel of the wicked
or stand in the way of sinners
or sit in the seat of mockers.
(Psalms 1:1)

Endnotes

1. Matthew 24:12
2. Revelation 12:15.
3. *Godliness Is Profitable,* Kenneth E. Haggin, ISBN 0-89276-256-X
4. *Even the Demons Believe,* by Timothy Williams, ISBN 1-57921-355-3
5. Mark 10:44
6. Philippians 2:6–7
7. 1 John 2:6
8. Luke 9:24
9. Revelation 2:14
10. Galatians 5:11
11. 1 Peter 4:1
12. Hebrews 2:8
13. Matthew 5:6
14. Luke 12:32–34
15. Proverbs 11:5
16. 2 Corinthians 1:5
17. Romans 8:36
18. 1 Corinthians 4:9
19. Revelation 7:16

20. Hebrews 11:39

21. John 15:19

22. James 4:4

23. John 15:19, Exodus 5:10

24. Exodus 10:21

25. Isaiah 5:20

26. Exodus 20:7

27. Psalms 132, See the book of Ecclesiastes

28. Deuteronomy 17:16–17

29. 1 Timothy 6:8

30. *Insanity in the Church,* by Timothy Williams, ISBN 1-57921-293-X

31. Moody Bible Institute had their bookstore filled with Jabez junk. Just to name one among many.

32. Psalm 73:9–12

33. *What Is Acceptable Music,* free tract available at www.sdoctrine.org

34. 2 Timothy 4:3

35. Michah 6:5

36. John 6:60

37. *Even the Demons Believe,* by Timothy Williams, ISBN 1-57921-355-3

38. James 1:27

39. Acts 16:14, 1 Corinthians 2:4–5

40. Acts 16:14, John 6:65

41. 1 Corinthians 3:7

42. 1 John 2:6

43. Mark 8:35, www.loserforjesus.org

44. Hebrews 3:8, Luke 8:13

45. Luke 8:13, Hebrews 3:8

46. 1 Corinthians 2:4

47. Books, tracts and advice from Larry Burkett, Ron Blue, Pat Robertson and many other "reasonable" money management experts have stopped the voice of the Holy Spirit and allowed the voice of the false prophet to grow louder and louder. It is easy to not appear greedy if we compare ourselves to the prosperity teachers rather than the words of Christ.

48. Matthew 14:17

49. Luke 12:34

50. Luke 14:33

51. 2 Corinthians 5:16

52. Matthew 7:5

53. James 4:3, 1 John 5:14–15

54. Luke 16:14

55. Luke 16:8

56. Acts 2:44

57. Acts 4:32

58. Acts 4:37, The first Christians didn't expand their territory, they sold it.

59. Luke 17:32

60. Request the free sermon, "The Jabez Delusion."

61. Jeremiah 23:14

62. Psalm 78:23–32

63. Jeremiah 17:9

64. 1 Peter 4:1

65. Philippians 2:20

66. 1 John 2:6

67. 1 Corinthians 2:2

68. Acts 20:35

69. Request the free sermon tape, "The Holy Spirit and Giving."

70. 1 John 2:6

71. Request the free sermon tape, "The Holy Spirit and Giving."

72. Luke 17:32

73. 1 Timothy 2:12, request the free sermon, "Women Preachers."

74. Keep your lives free from the love of money and be content with what you have, because God has said, "Never will I leave you; never will I forsake you." (Hebrews 13:5)

75. 1 Timothy 6:17, Proverbs 18:11, request the free sermon, "Message to the Rich"

76. Luke 14:33

77. John 12:25, Luke 14:25–35, Also see, *The Essential Piece* by Timothy Williams, ISBN 1-57921-293-X

78. Titus 1:16

79. 1 Peter 4:1

80. Titus 2:7, Preaching and teaching should reflect "seriousness" not joking or entertainment.

81. *Insanity in the Church,* by Timothy Williams, ISBN 1-57921-293-X

Other Books by Timothy Williams

Even the Demons Believe

- This book examines how Jesus made Christians while contrasting it with today's salvation calls. This book is a great tool for introducing non-believers to Christ, as well as giving Christians a fresh look at their salvation.
  ISBN: 1-57921-355-3

Insanity in the Church

- *Insanity in the Church* addresses the specific lies the church now regards as truth, making it ripe for the Powerful Delusion of the end times. Find out the only cure to the Powerful Delusion.
  ISBN: 1-57921-390-1

The Essential Piece

- This book examines why Jesus said anyone who follows Him must hate his own life.
  ISBN: 1-57921-293-X

A Whisper Revival

• This book explains how God wants to lead us to the "quiet waters" (Psalm 23:2) where we can honestly be revived. ISBN: 1-57921-274-3

101 Ways to Deny Self

• This book gives 101 practical ways in which to live out Jesus' command in Luke 9:23: Then he said to them all: "If anyone would come after me, he must deny himself . . ." ISBN: 1-57921-397-9

Bewitchment: You Foolish Galatians—The church of Christ and ICoC

• This book unmasks the problem of the International Church of Christ and the church of Christ, who both refuse to listen to the voice of the Holy Spirit by way of a crucified life. Find out the solution to this problem. ISBN: 1-57921-469-X

To order this book and others contact:

Sound Doctrine Ministries
PO Box 856
Enumclaw, WA 98022
email: sd@sdoctrine.org

or order online at: **www.thesaltshaker.com**
Honestly can't afford something? Contact us.

*O*rder your

free sermon

cassette tapes

entitled,

"The Balaam Series"

today.

To order contact us at

Sound Doctrine Ministries
PO Box 856
Enumclaw, WA 98022
sd@sdoctrine.org

Phone : (360) 825-4178

or order online at: www.freesd.org